Pottery:
Raku Technique

Pottery:
Raku Technique

Designs
Material
Technique

FINN LYNGGAARD

 VAN NOSTRAND REINHOLD COMPANY
New York   Cincinnati   Toronto   London   Melbourne

Van Nostrand Reinhold Company
Regional Offices:
New York Cincinnati Chicago
Millbrae Dallas
Van Nostrand Reinhold Company
International Offices:
London Toronto Melbourne

This book was originally published
in Danish under the title *Raku, ler,
glasur, braending* by J. Fr. Clausens
Forlag, Aschehoug, Copenhagen,
Denmark.

Copyright © 1970 by J. Fr.
Clausens Forlag. English translation
© Van Nostrand Reinhold Company
Ltd., 1973.

Library of Congress Catalog
Card Number: 72 12550
ISBN 0 442 29969 9

Translated from the Danish by
Joan Bulman.
Photography — Ole Woldbye,
Gunvor Jørgsholm and Finn
Lynggaard.

This book is printed in Great
Britain by Jolly and Barber Ltd.,
Rugby and bound by Henry Brooks,
Cowley, Oxford.

Published by Van Nostrand Reinhold
Company Inc. 450 West 33rd Street,
New York, N.Y. 10001 and Van
Nostrand Reinhold Company Ltd.,
25–28 Buckingham Gate,
London SW1E 6LQ.

Published simultaneously in Canada
by Van Nostrand Reinhold Company
Ltd.

16 15 14 13 12 11 10 9 8 7 6 5 4 3 2 1

Contents

Introduction

I hope very much that this book will encourage others to take up a branch of ceramic practice that has been forgotten or neglected for far too long: raku.

Like most present-day ceramic developments this aspect of the craft has its roots in Asia, having first appeared in Korea and China and then being developed by the skill of Japanese potters. But unlike earthenware, stoneware and porcelain, all of which have enjoyed a steady and continuing evolution both in Japan and in the rest of the world, raku has left no lasting traces in the ceramic art of the western world. Yet this simple technique brings ceramic production within the reach of everyone, and in spite of its modest demands in the way of technical equipment, provides a medium that offers astonishing possibilities to the creative artist.

Tea-bowl known as 'Fuji-san', by Honami Koetsu (1558–1637); diameter 4½ in (11·6 cm).

This book is addressed not only to the professional potter who is well versed in the mysteries of high temperatures, but also to the gifted amateur who, realizing his own limitations, seeks a style of pottery that will enable him to make his own ceramic pieces.

While working on this book I have not been able to shake off a slight fear that I should find myself at some stage or another in a Japanese blind alley, the whole thing seemed so firmly clamped in the Japanese tradition, but as the aim of the book was to recommend raku as a modern means of self-expression that would have been directly contrary to my intentions. I mentioned this problem to a Japanese potter and his answer was, that if we want to acquire any particular skill, and this applies just as much to modelling, decoration or calligraphy, the only thing we can do is to turn to those who have mastered it before us. By carefully studying and imitating their methods we shall have learnt enough in the course of a few years to begin to understand the artistic idea behind the technique and only then can we begin to think about expressing our own artistic intentions in this way.

I have therefore, in a spirit of the greatest respect for the mastery of the Japanese potters, deliberately slanted this book towards the Japanese raku tradition, in the hope that the reader will gain the necessary insight into the *technical* side of raku to enable him to discover new paths for himself.

What is raku?

In western ceramics in recent years there has been a steadily increasing tendency among potters to work with high temperatures, with stoneware and porcelain. The most delicate effects in clay and glaze are obtainable in this way and it is difficult to blame them if they occasionally lose their way among the labyrinthine opportunities open to them.

Very few potters have taken the opposite course – downwards in temperature to 750–800°C., and thus far below the normal earthenware level, which lies at about 1000°C. But there is a working area down here which, while making very modest demands in the way of technical equipment, opens up great possibilities for creative work. The tradition and history of the discipline have roots which are just as deep as those of the other schools of pottery on which we continue to build, but in one way or another this small and in its way restricted area has been completely by-passed.

Tea-bowl, Japanese
(c. 1800); (National
Museum, Copenhagen).

A primitive biscuit-firing kiln which consists simply of two loose protective walls with a covering of old kiln shelves.

This particular technique is known as raku. By raku is meant a low-fired, porous earthenware which is made of clay with a heavy content of grog and generally covered with a soft borax/lead glaze, after which it is fired by a special process in which the biscuit-fired, glazed article is placed in a red-hot kiln — 750—800°C. — and taken out again in a few minutes as soon as the glaze has melted. Heating and cooling consequently take place very suddenly, and the result is a brittle, porous product which has no actual functional value but which often has a simple beauty of its own. The demands made by raku are so simple that it can be practised with the aid of a provisionally built kiln which is heated up to red heat with wood fuel; the basic clay can be of almost any sort, and the composition of the glaze is the simplest imaginable.

The heavy grog content of the clay makes it unsuitable for large, complicated shapes, and even if a rich palette of coloured glazes is available, the best results will often be found among the less colourful and more unpretentious pieces.

The technical details will be dealt with more fully in their respective sections further on in the book, the following being only a general description of the making of raku.

Clay

The clay, which may be of any sort provided it has good plastic qualities, is mixed with a suitable quantity of grog, fireclay or sand so as to produce a body of sufficient porosity and with the necessary strength to be able to withstand the shock of heating and cooling during firing. The articles are shaped out of this clay by either throwing on the wheel or modelling, and when they are finished and completely dry they are fired in the normal way. The preliminary firing may be done in an ordinary ceramics kiln or in the actual raku kiln in which they will later be glost-fired. The temperature used for the preliminary firing should be a shade higher than for the glost-firing, in order to give the articles a reasonable mechanical strength; on the other hand the temperature must not be so high as to make glazing difficult and in no circumstances must there be any question of sintering of the body — the things then lose the capacity to be able to withstand the shock of heating and cooling and will explode as soon as they are placed in the kiln for glost-firing.

Glazes

After the preliminary firing the articles are glazed in the ordinary way and may be decorated either before or after this with under-glaze or overglaze colours. The glazes are uncomplicated combinations of lead or borax, or a number of ready-made products can be used. To ensure that the glaze binds on to the hard fired clay and to prevent it peeling off when put in the hot kiln, a small amount of binding material, such as gum arabic, a size made up from Carragheen Moss (Irish seaweed) or paperhanging paste is usually added to the glaze. After blending and straining, the glaze is applied in a thick, even layer either by dipping or by means of a brush, and the articles are set to dry out thoroughly before being placed in the kiln. It is essential that *all* the water in the glaze should be completely evaporated before this is done, since the slightest trace of moisture in the body will result in an immediate explosion when the articles are placed in the hot kiln. A pair of long-armed iron tongs is used to put the pieces in the kiln and the hands are protected with asbestos gloves; the kiln is shut and one can then watch through the peep-hole and see the glaze boiling up after a few minutes and melting, smoothing itself out to give an even surface. The whole thing takes only 10—15 minutes and as soon as it can be seen that the glaze is completely melted the kiln is opened again; the articles are taken out with the iron tongs and set to cool. During the swift cooling the glaze will almost always crackle and provided it has been laid on sufficiently thickly a harmonious line pattern will form which is characteristic of raku.

It stands to reason that a product which is the result of such a special firing technique will differ from other earthenware articles fired in a more traditional way, particularly as regards the strength and consequently the usefulness of the finished product. Raku articles will always be brittle and decidedly fragile; their 'usefulness' is limited to the pleasure to be found in making them and in looking at them afterwards.

A major attraction of the technique of raku is the exciting work-method involved, especially as so little is required in the way of tools, kiln and other equipment. Only the very simplest of tools are needed, and the firing can be done out of doors in a homemade kiln which is heated with wood refuse. Many will no doubt also value the companionship to be found in doing raku work, since it is far more speedily and easily carried out if there is a team of three or four.

Schools and raku

Many schools nowadays are well equipped with pottery rooms and expensive equipment for making ceramics, all of which comes under the heading of creative art. Even so, one is often shocked to discover how slender the results are, and it is particularly distressing to a professional potter to see the lack of understanding and the ill-informed attitude towards elementary ceramic processes that can result, for example, in the pupils being allowed to shape their own pieces of pottery which are afterwards fired by the teacher and the pupils finally painting the fired articles with gay poster paints.

The object of instruction in shaping articles in schools is not, of course, to train professional potters. But part of the object should be to give the children a feeling for a genuine piece of ceramic ware, and insight into the ceramic process with all the exciting possibilities in the way of clay, glaze and firing that it includes. The raku technique can give children a first-hand knowledge of the whole ceramic miracle, and the process will come home to them in a far more vivid way when they themselves can take part in it from A to Z. They will be thrilled by the quick results, in contrast to the usual system which has the great disadvantage that the time between the moment when the things are made until they are finished is very long.

Jar with alkali glaze, made
by Colin Kellam, England
(1969).

The origin and history of raku

Raku had its origins a long time ago, in early sixteenth-century Japan. Here, as in Korea and China, there was already a centuries-old ceramic tradition by this date; fine examples showing highly developed technical skill and outstanding artistic merit had already been known for many years. But owing to the social system then prevailing in Japan – a strongly feudal system with an enormous gap between the nobility and the simple peasantry – we know few of the names of these early potters. Their products were classified according to which 'kiln' they came from, and 'kiln' in this connection meant a geographical locality, in view of the fact that the trade of potter was connected with various areas of the country in which clay was of natural occurrence. Names such as Seto, Bizen, Kutani, Tamba, Shigaraki and many others all indicate such 'kilns' or ceramic centres. Within such a centre all the potters made the same local specialities; in one area it might be tea-bowls or water containers, in another flower vases or dishes. The individual potters seldom had their own kilns but fired their articles in the communal kiln together with their colleagues. Such communal kilns were wood-fired sectional kilns which might have up to twenty chambers and in these cases the potters would rent a definite space at each firing. They all helped one another with the filling and firing of the kiln – the last part of the process might take as long as a week. All this, together with their use of the same local supplies of raw materials in the form of clay and glaze, gave each area its peculiar local characteristics, and in spite of – or possibly because of – the constant repetition of simple forms with simple decorations, these everyday, practical articles often evolved into objects of great artistic skill and simple beauty. But it was in the nature of the social structure that common potters fell into the same class as peasants and artisans and as such were and remained anonymous.

Chojiro

Out of this anonymity a few names emerge at the beginning of the sixteenth-century. Chojiro (1516–92) was the son of the

brickmaker Ameya, an immigrant Chinese or Korean, who is said to have been the first to make ceramics of the kind that later came to be called raku. Chojiro continued his father's work in this technique and his unpretentious tea-bowls won especial favour with the contemporary masters of the tea ceremony; these were men of great influence and their protection will have played its part in drawing the potter out of his anonymity.

Tea-bowl, black raku, by Chojiro (1516–92); diameter $4\frac{1}{16}$ in (10·3 cm).

Raku, tea and Taoism

There is a close connection between raku, tea and Taoism which I can only lightly touch upon here. Tea drinking, which originally had a more ritual character and had been closely connected with the spread of Zen Buddhism, had acquired a more independent and worldly character by the beginning of the fifteenth-century. From being a rite it had become a ceremony, and in the tea ceremony we find the culmination of Japanese philosophy and aesthetics; a striving towards high ideals of harmony and simplicity. Special tea cults formed around the masters of the tea ceremony, the members of which endeavoured in every

Tea-bowl, black raku,
by Donyu (1599–1656);
diameter 4 $\frac{3}{16}$ in (10·7 cm).

branch of their lives to live up to certain standards in the combination of the useful and the beautiful. Both in the tea ceremony itself and in their daily lives they surrounded themselves with things that were simple, sober and unpretentious. The classical Japanese raku tea-bowl possesses these virtues and has the added advantage of being a poor conductor of heat.

Sen-no-Rikyu

The greatest and most influential master of the tea ceremony at this time was a man named Sen-no-Rikyu (1521–91), who valued Chojiro's work so highly that he presented him with a family name; Chojiro was called thereafter Tanaka Chojiro and regarded as the first raku (the word can also be used as a professional title) and the founder of the whole raku dynasty.

The raku symbol

The actual word raku comes from a Chinese ideogram, the meaning of which covers such concepts as: enjoyment, ease, pleasure, quiet and happiness. This ideogram was stamped on a gold seal which was presented in memory of Chojiro to his son, Jokei, by the feudal lord, Toyotomi Hideyoshi, and both the family and the technique have taken their name from the ideogram.

Jokei's son, Donyu (or Nonko, 1599–1656), continued the family tradition and we have some fine tea-bowls from his hand too, among which those in red raku (aka raku) have a peculiar charm.

One of Donyu's pupils was a gentleman-potter of the name of Honami Koetsu (1558–1637). He was originally a sword-maker by profession but like many other artists he also worked

Tea-bowl, black raku, known as Amagumo (rain clouds), by Honami Koetsu (1558–1637); diameter c. 4¾ in (12 cm).

17

in ceramics and some of the finest examples of raku can be ascribed to his rich talent. One of his best-known pieces is the tea-bowl illustrated elsewhere, which has become known as *Fuji-san* ('Venerable Fuji-mountain'); this bowl is registered in its homeland as a Japanese national treasure.

Momoyama and Edo

The raku technique has hardly found richer expression than in Kyoto during the so-called Momoyama period (1573–1615) and later the Edo period (1615–1867). An outstanding name of the latter period is that of Kenzan Ogata (1663–1743) whose masterly tea-bowls are a fine development of the raku tradition. The pieces he made were not restricted to tea-bowls, though these were particularly highly esteemed; he also exploited other possibilities with small rectangular and six-sided dishes which were often decorated by his elder brother, Korin Ogata (1658–1716), a greatly talented artist like Kenzan himself.

Square bowl by Kenzan Ogata (1663–1743); 8¾ × 8¾ in (22·2 × 22·2 cm).

18

From the Momoyama and Edo periods to present-day Japan there is an unbroken tradition of raku production, and the technique is continued in all essentials according to the same principles that were followed by these early masters. Notes and recipes have been handed down from generation to generation and even today there are direct descendants of the first raku: Raku Kichizaemon of Kyoto is the direct successor of Chojiro and works according to the notes and instructions left by him. A little while ago in my workshop I received a visit from Sen Soshitsu, who is the head of the Urasenke Tea Ceremony School, and as the fifteenth Sen the direct descendant of the famous Sen-no-Rikyu. Like his ancestor Sen Soshitsu, the fifteenth Sen is a man of tall stature and great artistic insight. In the course of our conversation about raku I had the opportunity of establishing that the present-day masters of the tea ceremony are also specialists in the matter of raku and of ceramic art in general.

Tea-bowl, red raku, by
Chojiro (1516–92);
diameter $4\frac{3}{32}$ in (10·4 cm).

'Night Child David', by
Jerry Threlkeld, U.S.A.
(1968).

Lead-glazed dish, 'Hare'
by Bernard Leach, England;
made in Japan (1919);
(National Craft Museum, Tokyo).

Raku outside Japan

For inexplicable reasons, however, the raku technique has never had any great following outside Japan. A certain number of potters have experimented with it at one time or another out of curiosity, but apart from that the whole thing has been regarded as, at best, a curious method of demonstrating and exemplifying a ceramic process, or, at worst, as something typically Japanese that is so rigidly hidebound as to leave no opportunity for fresh developments. Both attitudes are equally wrong; the former is based on ignorance, and as regards the latter, we should ask ourselves whether a great deal of our earthenware and stoneware production is not in fact based on Japanese traditions which we have contrived to develop and adapt to our own aesthetic and functional standards.

One of the few potters in the western world who has tried to treat raku as something more than just a curious phenomenon is Bernard Leach, in England. While visiting Japan in his youth Bernard Leach became a pupil of Kenzan Ogata the Sixth, from whom he inherited the title of Kenzan the Seventh, so that he has played his part in carrying on the tradition. Unfortunately he has only had very limited success with his attempts to introduce the technique into the western world.

Paul Soldner and Hal Riegger of the U.S.A. have worked exclusively for many years in the raku technique, to which they have given a completely personal expression. But apart from the artists mentioned and a very few others, it is as though a veil of oblivion had been drawn over this inspiring and exciting sphere of work.

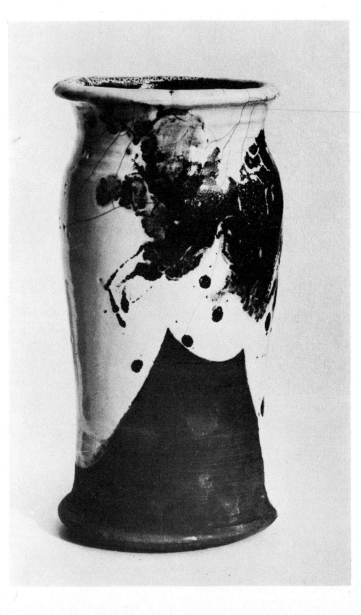

Jar by Phil Eagle,
U.S.A. (1968).

The raku technique

The raku technique will require something of an adjustment for most potters in that the whole process is different from that to which they are accustomed. Fortunately this adjustment is a matter of simplification so that it is not likely to cause anyone any difficulty. Clay, glaze and firing are so simple and uncomplicated that no difficulties will arise in the way of expensive technical equipment or extensive chemical knowledge. Obviously a technique as simple as raku sets certain limits as to what is possible, but far from deploring this fact I regard it as an advantage, in that the worker is confronted by quite elementary shaping and glazing problems. Raku can be regarded as a training and in particular as a training in moderation.

Clay – raku body

As an experiment I have tried altogether fourteen types of clay from different localities in Europe. This experimental material ranges from the most commonly known earthenware types through stoneware clay to porcelain clay. With a few reservations, connected in the main with the colour of the clay after the final firing, I believe that practically all types of clay can be used as raku clay. And that means that any local occurrence of more or less indeterminate composition can be used.

The only condition attached to raku clay is that in order to be able to resist the shock of heating and cooling it must have a high content of grog, fireclay, sand or some other coarse-grained material with qualities which will give the body sufficient porosity and fireproof qualities. Fireclay and sand usually have quite a fine-grained texture, which makes them less suitable than grog. If sand is used, red hill-gravel is preferable to sand from the sea-shore; the latter has a rounded structure which does not open up the body sufficiently.

Grog

As grog is in most cases already available at the workshop this will be the best additive to choose. The proportion of grog should not be less than 25 per cent and can be as high as 50 per cent of the finished clay. Rather than laboriously measuring out the dry ingredients most people will no doubt prefer to tip the powdered grog into the plastic clay and it will then be a question of intuition rather than of exact percentages; the principle will be to put as much grog into the clay as possible without making the clay impossible to shape. The grog will be easier to pour into the plastic clay if the powder is slightly moistened first with water.

The object of adding the grog is to obtain a sufficiently strong body by means of the fireproof quality of the grog, but strength will also depend on the coarseness of grain of the grog used, and thus the degree of porosity achieved. The smaller the size of grain of the grog, the less the porosity and the strength. The best results will be obtained with a grog with grains of 1–3 mm; if the clay is to be thrown however, the grog added to it should not have grains larger than 2 mm.

A body containing a load of coarse grog would make it lean and very difficult to throw. If clay for throwing is wanted it is therefore better initially to choose a basic clay which already has good plastic qualities, that is to say types of earthenware clay and to a certain extent stoneware clays. China clay must be regarded as less suitable and if a white ground is desired for purposes of decoration it will pay to use one of the first-mentioned types and cover it with a white clay where desired. Some types of earthenware clay, and this applies among others to red clays, take on a dead, greyish-red colour at the low firing temperature, which can however be to some extent counteracted by cooling under local reduction (see section on firing and cooling). But another method of dealing with this trouble is to add to the clay various easily fusible substances which are soluble in water; these will then blend during melting with a small proportion of the other constituents of the clay and give the fired body a warmer and softer character. Soda (sodium carbonate) in quantities of up to 4 per cent has this favourable effect and the solubility of the substance in water will result in an evaporation of soda from the interior of the body to the surface where the effect of the firing will be maximal. It is particularly emphasized that more than 4 per cent of soda must *not* be used; if it is the plastic structure of the clay will be altered, cf. soda in casting clay. Among other substances that may be used in this way are saltpetre (potassium nitrate), borax (sodium borate) or common cooking salt (sodium chloride). None of these substances should be added in quantities of more than 5–6 per cent; in larger quantities the alkaline substances can alter the superimposed layer of glaze.

Shaping

As has already been mentioned, the special character of the clay will have a considerable effect on the shaping possibilities. The low plasticity restricts throwing to simple and uncomplicated shapes, and it is no doubt for this reason that the tea-bowl or raku bowl has become the most popular raku product.

Nor is it difficult to understand why this particular shape has been and is so highly esteemed. In a modest shape of this sort some of the most elementary qualities of ceramics can be found — and some of the most difficult. Stripped of superfluities, ceramic expression is reduced to its basic constituents: shape, material, and colour. Whereas other, larger and more complicated shapes can impress simply by the technical perfection of shape or glaze, the humble raku bowl can display no such distracting side-effects: the demand for simplicity and harmony is inherent in the material and dictates the final result.

Unfired tea-bowl cut out of a lump of leather-hard clay. Particles of grog are exposed on the cut surfaces emphasizing the rustic and quite crude shape.

With practice it is possible to throw the coarse raku clay. For throwing small bowls it is a help to use a wooden 'former', as shown in this picture.

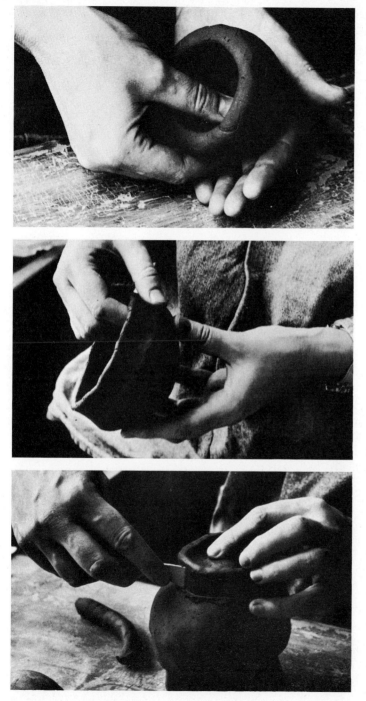

A raku bowl can be shaped out of a small lump of clay by pressing out a hollow in the clay with the ball of the thumb; the clay is then pressed with a rotating movement between the fingers until the walls of the bowl are of an even thickness. The warmth of the hands will draw out some of the moisture from the clay and dry it out — moisten the sides of the bowl from time to time with slip to prevent this.

When the bowl is shaped and has dried out for a few minutes until the clay is leather-hard, make a little roll of clay and fasten it with slip to the bottom to form a foot, shaping it with the fingers and with modelling tools.

The bowl shape

The bowl shape can be either hand-modelled or thrown but in either case the shape aimed at is simple and quite crude — crude in the sense of having no exaggerated finish. A further development of the basic shape towards an asymmetrical shape would be in line with the striving of raku towards the unpretentious and non-perfect. Perhaps this particular aspect of the aesthetics of the raku bowl will be difficult for many to understand; we westerners have been trained for centuries to think in terms of straight lines and geometrical curves so that any approach to the classical Japanese shapes *can* appear artificial and mannered. But in this connection one must never forget that raku, by its very nature, is an aesthetic form of ceramic production and that the fragile shapes will have no real functional value, but serve exclusively to give pleasure to the maker and the beholder. Apart from these criteria no limits can be set for what is allowed or not allowed in order to achieve the desired impression. Just as with us the pot shape has more or less thrown off its original function and become more of a sculptured shape, so the bowl shape can have its own aesthetic value which is not dependent on its usefulness.

Tea-bowl by Finn Lynggaard (1969). This shape is the so-called 'summer bowl', according to Japanese tradition. It is generally low and quite wide in contrast to the 'winter bowl' which is tall and cylindrical. (So that you can warm your hands on the hot bowl?)

Tea-bowl with Fujiyama
pattern. Japan, seventeenth
century. Mark: raku (family
mark). (*Property of the
Cultural Museum, Lund.*)

Foot and stamp of the
tea-bowl above. The
Japanese attach great
importance to the shaping
of the foot; great care is
given to this small detail
before the potter finally
puts his stamp on the
finished bowl.

Other shapes

So much for the raku bowl, but there are of course other possible shapes and as long as these are carried out in accordance with the limitations of the clay there is ample scope for imagination and development by the individual potter. Dishes, jars and combined, wheel-thrown pieces are suitable shapes, as are small sculptures and reliefs. One very important point to be remembered with any shape is that the thickness of the clay must be reasonably even so that the objects will be able to withstand the shock of the heat on being placed in the hot kiln; massive objects cannot be fired as raku. A thickness of $\frac{3}{16}-\frac{3}{4}$ in (0·5–2 cm) will have the best chance of surviving.

As raku kilns are generally quite small, this sets a limit to the size of the articles; remember that the pieces will have to be put into and taken out of the hot kiln with tongs and certain shapes can be decidedly awkward to handle.

Jar by Paul Soldner, U.S.A. (1967). The jar was partially glazed after the first firing, and slip-glazed. After the final firing the jar was locally reduced in a fire of grass.

Duck in the form of lidded pot. Lisa Engqvist (1951). During 1950–1 Lisa Engqvist worked for several periods with raku and some of the earliest examples of raku made by Danish potters are by her.

Figure by Birte Weggerby (1969).

Primitive biscuit-firing. The bowls are stacked on a pile of fire-bricks so as to leave air channels under the articles. Start by lighting small sticks of wood and afterwards, when the clay has completely dried out, larger and larger pieces of wood until the whole pile is thick with flames.

Overleaf:
Hot-water jar with lacquer lid, Mizusashi, Japan (eighteenth century). *(Museum of Industrial Art, Copenhagen).*

Preliminary biscuit-firing

If you already possess an ordinary pottery kiln, be it electric, gas or any other type, the obvious thing will be to do the firing in that. When the articles are well dried stack them in the kiln in the ordinary way and fire up normally. It is not even absolutely necessary for the clay articles to be completely dried out before being placed in the kiln; raku clay even at this stage has a very small coefficient of expansion and contraction and the risk of bursting is slight.

If you have no other kiln available than a homemade raku kiln the biscuit-firing may be done in that, but as the space inside the kiln is generally small it will perhaps be worth while building a rather larger kiln specially for this purpose. The biscuit kiln can be a temporary structure or just bricks piled up to fill an immediate need; kilns in the style of the old-fashioned charcoal kiln can also be used and in general demands are small provided a sufficiently high temperature is achieved so that the articles fired will be strong enough. Firebricks should be used to build a kiln rather than ordinary building bricks which crack after a single firing.

Biscuit-firing in a charcoal kiln or a homemade, wood-fired biscuit kiln will often result in a partial reduction of the body; this will be apparent in the form of dark-red or blackish patches according to the type of clay. These reduced areas will continue to be visible after the glazing and final firing of the article; the short firing period will not be enough to re-oxidize the clay

and the dark patches can help to give the articles a very interesting appearance similar to that obtained by local reduction during cooling.

Temperature

The temperature of the preliminary firing should be rather higher than that of the glost firing, that is to say, about 950–1000°C. for most types of clay; stoneware clay needs a rather higher preliminary firing temperature than earthenware clay. The temperature can be measured by pyrometers or cones; if such aids are not available the temperature can be judged by the colour of the interior of the hot kiln, which should be orange-yellow.

After the maximum temperature has been reached stoking is stopped and cooling takes place normally; if space is very limited, however, there is no reason why the articles should not be quickly cooled by removing them immediately from the kiln, and in the case of certain glazes it is an advantage to be able to glaze on to the still warm body to which a suitable layer of glaze is quickly applied.

Raku glazes

Raku glazes are just as simple and uncomplicated as the rest of the technique. A large number of different glaze effects and a wide range of colours can be achieved by very simple means. The successful product will be not so much the result of complicated chemical combinations as of the richly varied possibilities offered by the special firing and cooling techniques.

Classical glazes

Classical raku glazes, i.e. glazes made from recipes which have been handed down from early raku potters, are designed for temperatures around 750–800°C. and may be made up as the following two examples:

a)	b)
60 g Lead carbonate	70 g Lead carbonate
20 g Quartz	23 g Quartz
20 g Frit	7 g Shiratama
(Leach)	(Kenzan/Tomimoto)

Frits and shiratama in the two examples mean the same thing, namely a powdered frit consisting of 50 per cent lead carbonate, 39 per cent quartz, 11 per cent calcinated borax. Experimenting with the above glazes I have tried, for lack of anything better, replacing the frits/shiratama with, among other things, lead bisilicate, borax frit and commercially manufactured ground glass;

all with more or less the same results as regards melting qualities. A warning concerning raku glazes made on a basis of lead carbonate is that the material is difficult to make up with water into a paste and it is *poisonous* (as is red lead) and so should never be used in schools or in any form of instruction. Even when the greatest care is taken all forms of lead may be absorbed by the organism through the respiratory system of the skin, and may cause prolonged poisoning or even disablement.

Frits

So far as is possible one should avoid using lead products and as there is fortunately a large selection of ready-made frits available in which lead is present in a non-poisonous form, this will not present any great problem. In fact, there are great advantages in using these ready-made frits in that they boil up less during firing than the raw lead glazes; the finished product obtained is far better melted and in addition one is saved the bother of

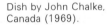
Dish by John Chalke, Canada (1969).

calculating and weighing out a number of substances. Ready-made frits obtainable are lead-, lead/borax-, borax- or alkali-frits and it is up to the individual to choose which type he prefers. The important thing when purchasing a frit is to make sure that it is intended for the desired temperature and that any addition of colouring metal oxide will have the effect intended. Lead frits have a tendency to become shiny and they reduce badly, whereas borax glazes have a duller shine and the colours in this case are clearer and purer. Frits may be used in a pure form without the addition of other substances or they can be made opaque or varied in colour as desired.

As mentioned elsewhere, the word raku can also refer to a style, and that is the case with the stoneware bowl shown here. Apart from the material and the firing technique the bowl has the characteristic 'primitive' appearance of raku. Japan, eighteenth century, mark: raku. (*Museum of Industrial Art, Copenhagen*).

Opaque and coloured glazes

The addition of 3–5 per cent tin oxide to most glazes will make the glaze whiter and more opaque. For coloured glazes the metal oxide content can be quite large in comparison with glazes for higher firing temperatures. The table below shows within which intervals the colour indicated is generally obtained with the commonest metal oxides:

Right
Figure, by Jeppe Hagedorn-Olsen (1969).

      3–8%   Iron oxide   light to dark brown
      2–6%   Copper oxide   turquoise
      0·5–2% Cobalt oxide   light blue to bluish black
      1–3%   Manganese dioxide   violet to reddish brown

  A combination of several oxides is possible and a number of different tones can be produced in this way, as e.g.

$$\left.\begin{array}{ll} 2\% & \text{Cobalt oxide} \\ 6\% & \text{Iron oxide} \\ 4\% & \text{Manganese dioxide} \end{array}\right\} \text{black}$$

I have used the following frits as a starting point for glaze building, all of which fulfil the requirements for easy fusibility:

Podmore & Sons Ltd:
  Borax frits P 2245
  Lead frits P 2241 Lead Bisilicate — P 2242 Lead
    sesquisilicate
  Alkali frits P 2250 High Alkali frit

Harrison Mayer Ltd:
Soft Borax frit

Of these the borax frits in particular have proved suitable for the addition of colouring metallic oxides, while the lead frits give good results over slips or underglaze colours.

Other types of glaze

With earlier potters' glazes as a starting-point it is possible to make glazes with proportional mixtures of red lead and clay. These glazes have a very pleasing quality and the tendency will be towards half-matt, half-transparent tones ranging from whitish grey to light brown according to which clay was used in the glaze or as a base. An earthenware clay with a relatively low melting point should always be used, and the following could serve as a rough guide:

50 g Red lead
50 g Red clay or pipeclay

The addition of colouring metallic oxides to this glaze will be made in accordance with the standards given above.

If one wishes to avoid using poisonous red lead an equally simple glaze can be obtained with calcium borate as flux. The character will be rather different on account of the borax content and the colours will appear clearer and purer.

The proportions should be changed to the following:

75g Calcium borate
25g Red clay or pipeclay

Remember with this type of glaze that calcium borate quickly thickens ('calcifies') after mixing and that it is not worth while making up more glaze than one wants for immediate use.

A number of metallic oxides have a tendency to lose the strength of the colour as the temperature rises and it is well known that, for example, stoneware glazes are often very restrained and quiet in appearance. But with the low firing

temperature used in the raku technique it is possible to obtain strong, vital colours which would disappear under different, higher firing conditions. Even if it harmonizes badly with the demand of raku for 'the simple and unassuming', it is worth mentioning that the metallic oxides of uranium, cadmium, selenium and others can give strong orange and red colours. The same applies to chromium oxide which in combination with certain lead glazes can turn red and give orange-coral red colours. A chromium-red glaze can have the following composition:

114 g	Red lead
15 g	Quartz
13 g	Kaolin
3·8 g	Chromium oxide

The intensity of the colour is increased if the glaze is used on a white body or a light slip.

Besides the examples of glazes mentioned here there are any number of others which are just as practicable. If one starts with the basic principle that the glaze must consist of an easily melted flux plus a stabilizer, it will be relatively simple to produce new and exciting results. The flux can be any easily melted material such as red lead, lead carbonate, calcium borate, lithium carbonate, commercial ground glass or many others, and substances such as clay, ochre, quartz, kaolin or others which will similarly give the glaze substance can be used as stabilizers. In test-firing new glazes mark with chromium oxide the clay substances which are not affected by firing or by possible local reduction during cooling.

Tea-bowl by Ryozo Miki (1969). The Japanese bowl has two basic forms one of which, like the one shown here, is quite tall with a cylindrical shape and is known as a 'winter bowl'. The other basic shape, the 'summer bowl', is low and open.

Right
Incense holder in the form of a dragon. Mark: Ninsei. Kogo/Kyoto, Japan. *(Property of the National Museum.)*

Examples of glazes

I have collected from various sources a selection of recipes for glaze which might serve as a basis for the individual potter's experiments:

1)   55 g Lead carbonate
      25 g Quartz
      10 g Felspar
       5 g Clay
       5 g Chalk
           (Rhodes)

2)   60 g Red lead
      40 g Quartz
      10 g Borax
          (Green)

3) 100 g Carbonate of lead
      40 g Quartz
         (Kenzan)

4) 100 g Carbonate of lead
      35 g Borax frit
      25 g Quartz
         (Kenzan/Oshikoji)

5)   50 g Carbonate of lead
      30 g Borax frit
      15 g Quartz
       5 g Nepheline syenite
         (Riegger)

6)   80 g Colemanite (borate of calcium)
      20 g Felspar
         (Soldner)

7)   30 g Colemanite (borate of calcium)
      20 g Kaolin
      10 g Quartz
         (Soldner)

Tea-bowl by Lene B. Kristensen (1969). The bowl is made in red raku clay and the glaze, which is light yellowish-brown, is based on red lead and clay.

Opposite
Temporary preliminary firing kiln of ordinary building bricks. It is fired from below with dry wood and the vertical channel acts both as chimney and kiln chamber. We measured a temperature of about 650°C. at the top of this kiln with a pyrometer after 2–3 hours' firing.

Black raku

The black raku glaze occupies a special position among glazes, and is rather different from those already mentioned. The body in this case must be a stoneware clay with a large percentage of grog — 35–40 per cent — and the firing must be done at about 1150–1200°C.; the ordinary raku kiln cannot therefore be used and the firing is often done in a smallish stoneware kiln.

The main ingredient of the original black raku glaze is a kind of rock known as Kamogawa-ishi, containing iron and manganese which give the special colour. A black glaze which is reminiscent of the original can be made up as follows:

        50 g Red lead
        38 g Quartz
        12 g Kaolin
         9 g Iron oxide
        3·5 g Manganese dioxide

One condition for getting the right colour is that the cooling must be done by plunging the article ruthlessly into a pail of lukewarm water, as soon as it comes out of the hot kiln. This must be done quickly as if it is allowed to cool off more slowly the glaze will change colour from black to reddish-brown. The right colour will in some cases only be obtained by the repeated glazing and firing of the same article. This can be repeated up to five or six times, when a 'curtain-like' pattern will be produced by the flowing of the glaze.

Tea-bowl, black raku by Donyu (1599–1656) with donyu mark; diameter 4 $\frac{1}{16}$ in (10·3 cm).

40

Jar by Finn Lynggaard
(1969).

Glazing

Irrespective of whether one chooses the one type of glaze or the other, it is important that the glaze should be applied to the clay article in a suffciently thick layer. Articles too thinly glazed will have an uneven appearance that spoils the thing as a whole, whereas an even, thick layer of glaze will give the form a gentle, pleasing quality that makes it pleasant to touch. The rapid firing process will prevent even a very thick layer of glaze from causing damage in the kiln by running or dripping down.

When blending the materials for the glaze add to the mixing water a small quantity of binding agent which can be gum arabic, a size made up from Carragheen Moss (Irish seaweed) or ordinary wallpaper adhesive (cellulose). This is to prevent the glaze peeling off when placed in the hot kiln and at the same time the binding agent will prevent the frit or heavy particles in the glaze from sinking to the bottom; the glazed article will also stand handling better before it is placed in the kiln.

After making up the liquid the whole is passed through a fine-meshed sieve in order to ensure a thorough mixing of the constituents and an equal consistency throughout. If necessary a little more water is added to produce the desired viscosity and the glaze can then be applied either by dipping, pouring, spraying or with a brush.

When the clay article has been glazed it is set to dry out thoroughly before being placed in the kiln. Even the slightest trace of unevaporated water in the body will inevitably result in a violent explosion when the article is placed in the kiln. Articles can be dried out and warmed by being placed on top of the kiln before they are fired.

Jar with black lustre-glaze by Finn Lynggaard (1969). Through local reduction the black glaze has taken on a rich play of red, blue and violet shades with a metallic glint that can be imagined from the photograph.

Square lidded jar, by Birte Weggerby (1969).

Kilns

It is obvious that a kiln which is only required to reach the relatively low temperature, about 800°C., at which raku glaze melts, need be nothing elaborate. In most cases it is possible to manage with homemade structures, which may either be of a more permanent nature or simply a primitive kiln of piled bricks to cover an immediate need.

A great deal of scope is left to the individual imagination and raku kilns can be constructed in many different ways. No one type is to be preferred to any other so long as the desired temperature is obtained within a reasonable period of time and with the supplies of fuel available.

The traditional kiln

The traditional raku kiln is a wood-fired brick construction like the one shown here:

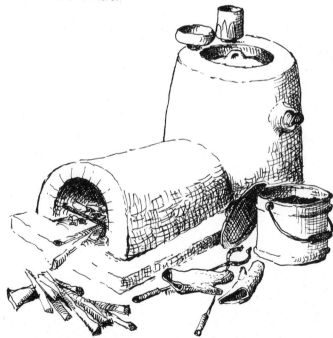

The traditional raku kiln can be built of moler or fireclay bricks. To support the arched structure of the firing channel a framework of cardboard or veneer is used which is drawn out through the opening in front once the bricks are firmly in place. Finally a layer of mortar is spread over the kiln which, if it is mixed with a little cement, not only serves to give the rounded form but also provides a certain protection against wind and weather.

43

Section of kiln. Building the kiln on a foundation of concrete slabs prevents the moisture in the earth from rising up into the porous moler bricks.
Notice the three iron bars in the firing channel and also the built-in support stones for the muffle (see also ground plan).

Ground plan.
The firing channel narrows in slightly towards the kiln chamber, from which the heat is distributed up round the sides of the muffle. The distance from the muffle to the sides of the chamber should be $1\frac{1}{2}$–2 in (4–5 cm).

Cardboard or veneer framework for use in bricking over the firing channel.

The firing is done through the channel at the bottom and the heat is conducted from there up into the chamber of the kiln itself, which is shaped rather like a wide chimney. Inside the 'chimney' rests a muffle made of fireclay, in which the glazed article is placed during firing. The use of this inside capsule or muffle reduces the loss of heat through repeated opening and closing of the kiln; floating ash will not be able to settle on the glaze, which is also reduced less violently than if it were fired without a muffle. Even with firing in a muffle, however, there will always be a certain amount of reduction which will have an effect on both clay and glaze. Since the reducing kiln atmosphere will in the majority of cases add essential qualities to both clay and glaze, it should be added here that the use of a muffle is by no means essential for good results. On the contrary, reduction carried out during the actual firing will be far more permanent than superficial local reduction, and this latter method will therefore be mainly used in connection with firing in electrical kilns, where it is not possible to control the atmosphere of the kiln.

The kiln shown here is built of moler bricks which are stacked up without mortar, the bricks being kept in place by their own weight. If one wishes to improve on this structure the bricks can be built up with a mortar consisting of equal quantities of fireclay and lime mortar. Joints and spaces between the bricks can be filled up with this mixture and finally the whole outside of the kiln washed over with a layer of liquid mortar. A further strenghtening would be achieved by fixing two or three iron bands round the cylinder to prevent it cracking.

Raku kiln of moler bricks. The model shows how the bricks are stacked and held in place by their own weight. Improvements could consist in building the wall with mortar and a better firing would undoubtedly be obtained by making the firing channel longer and wider.

Bowl with milk-white lead glaze, Walter Keeler, England (1969).

Thrown muffle of raku clay.

The muffle

The muffle is a cylindrical container which is about 9¾ in (25 cm) high and about the same in diameter. As it will be exposed to intense direct heat it should be of good fireproof quality. Muffles of carborundum can be bought which are very strong, but they have the disadvantage of being quite expensive so that it will generally be worth while to make a muffle oneself. For this purpose use a clay consisting of equal quantities of fireclay, stoneware clay and coarse grog (⅛ in; 3 mm). This mixture will be very non-plastic and consequently difficult to throw. Anyone not sufficiently experienced at throwing can model a muffle instead, over a framework of cardboard or veneer. Roll a long strip of cardboard or thin veneer into a cylinder, fastening the edges where they overlap with a clip or clamp. The framework must be slightly higher than the final muffle to allow room for the clamp. Build a cylinder round this framework with a suitable layer of clay about ¾ in (2 cm) – and when the clay starts to shrink as it dries, reduce the diameter of the framework from time to time to prevent the clay cracking. Remove the framework in any case as soon as the clay is strong enough to hold, that is, when it approaches the leather-hard stage. This is also the right moment to give the cylinder a bottom; a round sheet of clay rolled out with a rolling-pin to a thickness corresponding to the wall of the cylinder – the clay cylinder is placed on top of the sheet of clay, and the two joined together with slip.

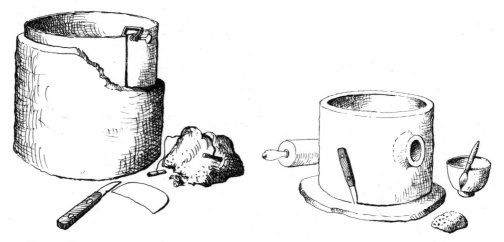

The muffle must be provided with a lid with a handle or lug so that it can be lifted on and off with an iron hook. A muffle lid can be made without turning by laying a round sheet of clay the same diameter as the muffle to dry over a heap of grog or sand. When the sheet is leather-hard give it a strong lug or handle.

The left hand sketch shows the cardboard cylinder with the clay starting to be built up round it. The top is straightened off with a knife or wire. The right hand sketch shows the mounting of the finished cylinder on the bottom plate. After joining together with slip, any superfluous clay is removed with a knife.

Section of raku kiln with round flue. To obtain a comfortable working height the kiln is built on a foundation of porous concrete with a layer of concrete slabs on top. As is shown in the sketch the muffle rests on a 'shelf', which can be an ordinary kiln shelf placed so as to leave a suitable space behind it, where heat can pass through into the kiln chamber. The muffle is raised a few centimetres on a pile of bricks so that the heat can act on it on all sides.

The traditional raku kiln is heated with dried wood split in pieces $1\frac{1}{4}$–$1\frac{3}{4}$ in (3–4 cm) thick. It is stoked continuously with two or three sticks to obtain a steady rise in temperature and when after 2–3 hours the muffle is red hot the kiln will have reached a temperature of about 750–800°C. and glaze firing can begin. See further details in the section on firing (pp 62–4).

A kiln of the type sketched above has been used for centuries

Section of coal/coke kiln.
The hatched areas indicate
firebricks and the dotted
areas moler bricks or other
insulating bricks. The cover
is cast of some fireproof
material which is obtainable
commercially; enquire
further of kiln builders.

Plan of kiln.
The sketch shows how the
muffle is suspended on
three supporting bricks, also
the link through the wall
of the kiln with the peep-
hole in the muffle.

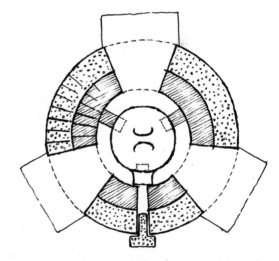

Page 49
Round up-draught kiln.
Glazed bowls are set to
dry on top of the hot kiln;
the four vent holes can be
seen above the firing
chamber. If the firing
channel is too short
unburnt gases will pour
out here and may catch
fire. This means poor use
of fuel and to improve
matters the firing channel
must be made longer so
that the gases burn inside
the kiln.

by Japanese raku potters for making ceremonial tea-bowls. The
kiln was rarely expected to hold more than at most two or three
bowls at any one time, but this very fact ensured the wealth
and variety of design.

Improvements on this same type of kiln can be worked out on
this basis, but it must always be borne in mind that the size of the
kiln and the thickness of the insulating bricks must bear some
reasonable relationship to one another; as soon as you go beyond
the size of muffle shown here, another half brick's insulation
would be necessary in order to maintain a constant temperature.
It is therefore usually better to choose a rather different type of
kiln, e.g. the coal- or coke-fired kiln.

Bowl by Finn Lynggaard (1969).

Tea-bowl, Japan.
Inscription, a haiku, which in
English means:
*One sip of the tea one touch
of the hand will bring
renewed life. Kenzan
copies this.*

Tea-bowl with Fujiyama
decoration. Mark: Dohashi.
Kyoto, Japan (eighteenth
century). *(Museum of
Industrial Art, Copenhagen.)*

Tea-bowl, Japan (*c.* 1790);
Riunyu? *(Museum of
Industrial Art,
Copenhagen.)*

Coal- and coke-fired kilns

A kiln which in principle resembles the wood-fired one can be
used with little alteration for coal- or coke-firing. The fuel value
is greater with these products than with wood and a more
constant heat is obtained with less labour.

The essential difference is that the coke-fired kiln is not fired
from the bottom only, but through the top opening. The firing
channel is replaced by three stoke-holes, all of which are fired
during the first stage; at a later stage they serve as ash-doors for
the removal of ash and slag.

The muffle may be up to 16 in (40 cm) high and the same in
diameter. A muffle made of carborundum is preferable in this
case as the direct heat from the surrounding coal or coke can
cause a weaker muffle to become distorted. The kiln is heated
by stoking at first only through the three stoke-holes at the bottom, and then, as soon as there is a good fire there, stoking from
above with coal or coke. Gradually fill up with coal or coke to
the top rim of the muffle, scraping the red-hot coals together

Lead-glazed jar by Harry Horlock Stringer, England (1969). The decoration is done by the 'wax-resist' method and after reduction in peat-dust the unglazed parts appear as dark patches.

at regular intervals with an iron rod so that the ash and slag falls down to the bottom of the kiln, from where it can be removed through the stoke-holes. Economic use will be made of the fuel if this type of kiln is built with a surround of insulating bricks and an inner casing of firebricks. The innermost layer (half a brick thick) must be of high-fired firebricks while the insulating outer layer ($\frac{1}{2}$ brick thick) can consist of moler bricks or similar insulating bricks.

Quite high temperatures can be reached with this kiln, up to 1100°C., and in a larger size it will serve admirably as a general earthenware kiln. In this case the lid of the muffle must be provided with a peep-hole and a Seger cone must be placed immediately under it, for judging the temperature of the kiln.

Gas-fired kilns

A gas-heated raku kiln will be the most practical and effective where there is any question of a more continuous production of raku articles. A temperature of up to 800°C. can be obtained in the space of quite a short time and by regulating gas and air a constant temperature can be maintained, which means that each firing will take at most 5–10 minutes.

A gas kiln, heated with Calor gas, can be built in much the same way as the wood-fired kiln but in this case the firing channel does not need to be so long as no space is needed for a fire. The kiln can be heated with a simple gas burner which is placed in the middle of the stoke-hole opening and built in with bricks and mortar. If the firing can be done without any extra supply of air, by means of a blower or compressed air installation, a certain amount of reducing atmosphere will be produced automatically in the kiln and at the same time the heat will last longer.

A compressed air or blower installation would, however, be too complicated for most people to install for themselves, so we recommend consulting an expert in these matters.

The principle of the gas-fired kiln is the same as for the traditional, wood-fired kiln; but the firing chamber is smaller as shown here. A firebrick is stood at a slant in front of the burner to throw the flame up, under and round the muffle. The kiln is built of firebricks and can have an insulating lid of moler bricks.
A = air, B = gas.

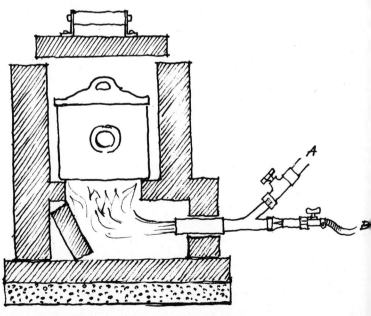

Working with a home-made bank kiln is an exciting occupation, especially for children.

Bank kilns or climbing kilns

A bank, or climbing, kiln is a very simple but none the less very effective type of kiln. It consists simply of a firing tunnel and a kiln chamber/ventilation shaft which is dug into a slope or the side of a hill. The firing tunnel must be about 40 in (1 m) long, and a ventilation shaft which is at the same time the actual kiln chamber is dug from the bottom of the tunnel vertically upwards. A muffle is inserted into this space and apart from this the firing procedure is the same as for the wood-fired kiln.

Before starting to excavate a kiln of this sort it would be worth while investigating the quality of the soil. The kiln will be firmer if it is excavated in a clay or heavy soil whereas a sandy bank is less suitable, the whole thing will simply collapse as soon as the earth dries out.

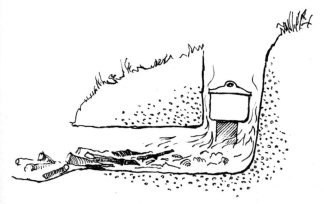

The bank kiln must be the cheapest kiln it is possible to build. It consists really of just a couple of holes in the ground, but in spite of its simple construction it is extremely effective.

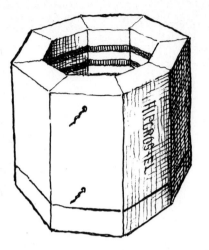

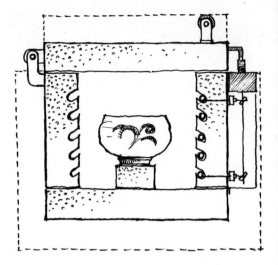

Electric raku kiln of
high-insulating bricks.

Section of electric raku kiln.
The dotted line indicates a
possible insulating layer of
moler brick which would
increase efficiency.

Electric kilns

And finally you can of course use an ordinary electric kiln of
suitable size, such as a small test kiln or a frit kiln. The only
drawback with electric kilns is that they can only be used for
firing with an oxidizing kiln atmosphere, but this difficulty can
to some extent be remedied by cooling the article under local
reduction as described under firing.

Before beginning to use an electric kiln one should remember
one very important thing: it is highly dangerous to use an electric
kiln for raku firing unless the kiln is provided with a door contact
which automatically breaks the current when the door is opened.
It is no use thinking that it will be enough just to be careful,
or rely on turning a wall switch on and off; that is all too easily
forgotten in the hectic speed of the work and the only effective
safeguard is to see that the current is automatically cut as soon as
the kiln door is opened. A further safeguard would be if the
electric kiln was provided with a muffle of fireclay which covered
the heating elements so that it was impossible to touch them.
This would also have the advantage that they could not be
damaged by pottery which happened to burst in the kiln. All
too often glazed articles are not sufficiently dried out before being
placed in the kiln, so that they burst into thousands of fragments
a few seconds after being put inside. Fragments of clay or glaze
which are deposited on the heating elements will cause these to
fuse or break in a very short time.

The electric raku kiln can, up to a point, be made at home by
anyone with a flair for these things. But by 'up to a point' I
mean everything except the electrical fittings and the installation
of these, which should always be left to an expert. In any case it
must always be checked by the Electricity Board.

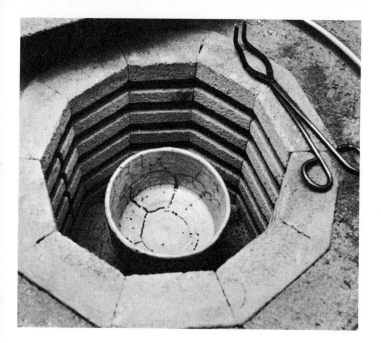

The structure of the chamber of an electric kiln is shown in this picture. The bricks are sawn off at an angle so that eight or, as here, ten bricks form the sides of the kiln. Grooves are sawn or filed into the bricks to take the electric wires.

Electric kiln of highly porous brick with an insulating coat of fireclay.

The kiln can be built of light firebricks — e.g. a quality like Hiporos-El, the one in the diagram — and the construction can be as shown on p. 54. The bricks are sawn so that eight form the actual chamber of the kiln. After fitting the bricks together saw or file a groove for the heating element, on the side facing inwards. Two holes must be bored in the top or bottom groove for the two ends of the heating element. The bottom also consists of firebricks which are fitted to the shape of the kiln, after which all the bricks can be held together with a thin layer of fireproof mortar. To give the kiln greater strength and make it portable the whole thing can be packed in a layer of aluminium foil (about $\frac{1}{16}$ in or 1·5 mm) and bound round with a couple of iron bands. The lid is also made of firebricks held together with an iron band and with a handle on top made of insulating material such as asbestos. On the side of the cover a metal arm is fixed which when the lid is closed activates a contact on the kiln itself and so closes the current.

The heating element consists of a coiled resistance wire (e.g. Kanthal A) and for a kiln of this sort 120 ft (36 m) Kanthal, diameter $\frac{1}{16}$ in (1·7 mm). The wire is twisted with an internal diameter of $\frac{5}{16}$ in (8 mm) and after twisting the wire is stretched to a suitable length to fill the groove. The ends of the wire are carried out through the holes at the top and bottom and connected with the door contact and also with the wall contact. Kilns which are mounted in a metal frame or aluminium foil must be provided with an earth contact but all this, as stressed above, should preferably be entrusted to an authorized fitter.

As a curiosity we have shown on the opposite page a wheel-thrown raku kiln. The kiln is made of fireclay in sections which are locked together with a running natch. The kiln was made as a portable model like the kilns that were used by the Japanese potters at raku tea ceremonies. Owing to the thinness of the insulating layer the heating-up time is very long and the kiln must be regarded as decorative rather than functional.

Sketch showing the division of the thrown raku kiln into sections and the structure in general.

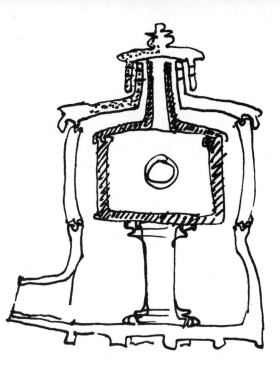

Raku kiln thrown in sections.

Tea-bowl by Finn Lynggaard (1969). The decoration is executed as glaze on glaze and one can see how the dark, superimposed glaze has run to form a soft festoon.

For local reduction, after being taken out of the kiln the fired article is plunged immediately into a metal container full of inflammable material such as wood-wool, hay, straw or dead leaves.

For inserting and removing a pair of long-handled iron tongs is used, the ends of which are shaped so that they will grip the bowl firmly without any danger of damaging the edge.

The red-hot bowl is taken out of the kiln.

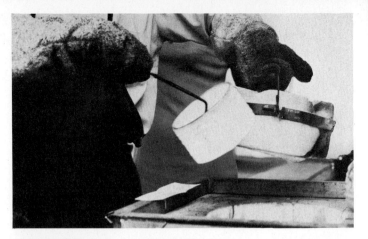

After only a few seconds the outside of the bowl begins to cool, so if any local reduction is desired it must be seen to *now*.

Meantime, other glazed bowls have been dried and warmed on top of the kiln; as soon as a bowl is removed one of these is placed in the kiln and the process continues.

Opposite
A radical method of cooling consists in dipping the red-hot bowl in cold water immediately it has been removed from the kiln.

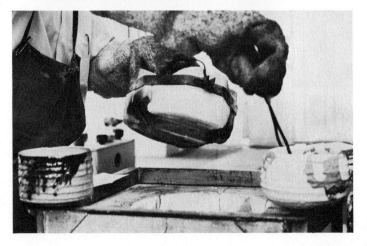

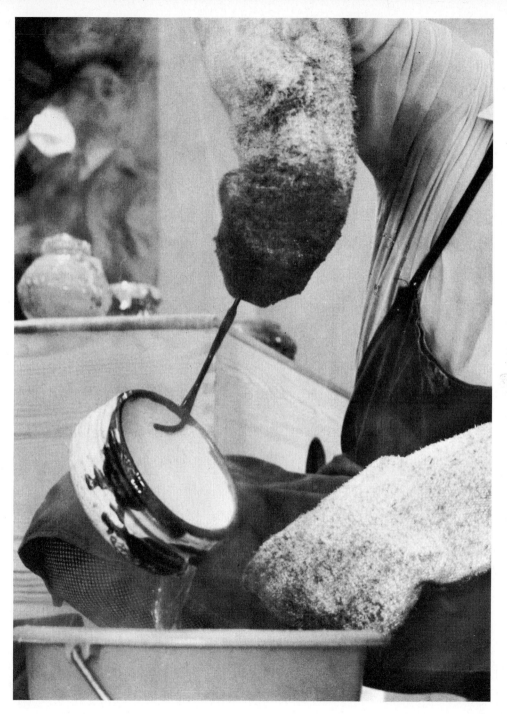

Firing

And now we have reached the most exciting part of the whole procedure: the firing. There is something enormously fascinating about being able to put a glazed clay article into a red-hot kiln and then, a few minutes later, taking the finished product out of the kiln again. And moreover, this is not just some poor imitation or something that merely looks like ceramics, but a genuine ceramic product that has gone through the normal procedure for clay and glaze in record time. It is during this stage of the raku process that the tempo can become a trifle hectic since the kiln must be watched over all the time and must be constantly emptied and filled again. And nothing can really be compared with the terrific joy one feels every now and then when some particular piece comes out of the kiln with all the qualities which one has been striving for, warmth, excellence and beauty.

To return to the hard facts a group with at least two and preferably more team members makes the work a good deal easier. The stoking of a fuel-fired kiln alone is enough to keep one man busy and it would be an advantage to have two people to open and fill or empty the kiln.

62

The heating up of the kiln should be done in the case of all fuel-fired types sufficiently slowly not to crack the muffle. When the heating has gone on for about half an hour stoking can be speeded up until finally the muffle is red hot and firing can begin. The glazed articles have already been thoroughly dried out and warmed and, using a pair of long iron tongs and wearing asbestos gloves to protect the hands, a glazed article is now placed inside the muffle, where it is stood on a sheet of asbestos or fireclay to prevent it fusing to the bottom. The muffle is closed as quickly as possible after the article has been placed inside and if the kiln is provided with a peep-hole one can watch through that how the glaze starts melting almost at once. It will bubble and boil and then within 10–15 minutes smooth itself out again and form an even surface. When this point seems to have been reached the muffle is opened again and the article taken out. In doing so it is unavoidable that the iron tongs should leave marks in the still soft surface of the glaze, but this one simply has to accept as something that is characteristic of raku. If the glaze turns out to be not completely melted (and it may be difficult to judge the

If after glost firing the article appears not to have reached a sufficiently high temperature – or quality – there is nothing to prevent glazing and firing it again.

red-hot product at first) it can be returned to the kiln and refired; or it can be coated first with a fresh layer of glaze and can be refired five or six times before the clay becomes so 'fatigued' that in the end it simply cracks.

Cooling

After the fired article has been taken out of the kiln one can choose between various different methods of cooling, and it should be emphasized that this part of the process is by no means the least important.

If the red-hot article is cooled in the normal way, by being placed to cool on a fireproof base, you will obtain an oxidized product in which the glaze and decorative colours will correspond to what is normally obtained from the various colouring oxides: copper will give green or greenish-blue shades, cobalt a vivid blue and iron reddish-brown colours, and so on. This method of cooling is therefore particularly suitable where it is intended to achieve definite colour effects and where decoration proper is concerned. It is extraordinary to watch the red-hot article as it slowly cools and the colours changing meanwhile from glowing reddish-gold until the final colours gradually appear. Even after the sides of a bowl have cooled and taken on the intended colour there will be a glowing red patch at the bottom of the bowl and this forms an exciting contrast to the rest.

Local reduction

There is one method of cooling which gives a final product that is perhaps most in keeping with the whole idea of raku. This method is known as local reduction and the meaning of the term is that a delayed reduction of the still red-hot glaze takes place after the article has been taken out of the kiln. In practice this means that the red hot article, *immediately* after being removed from the kiln, is placed in a metal container full of inflammable material such as wood-wool, sawdust, and straw. The container is closed with a closely fitting lid and a firing now takes place which has a reducing character owing to the lack of oxygen. If the inflammable material is moistened with water first the reducing effect will be still greater, but on the other hand a great deal of smoke will be given off and it is recommended that this process should be undertaken only out of doors. When the article is taken out of the container a few minutes later a distinct change will be seen in clay and glaze. As far as the glaze is concerned the reduction will cause a chemical reaction in the metallic oxides which will be particularly apparent in the colouring metallic oxides; cobalt will be changed to a softer tone of blue, iron will in some cases take on greenish tones and copper will become red instead of green. As the results of this procedure are very uncertain it cannot be foretold in each individual case what the final colour will be, and the same glazes will give different results on different occasions. Glazes with a large content of colouring oxides, and this applies particularly to copper oxide, will have a tendency to take on a metallic sheen; thus glaze or decorative colours will take on an appearance similar to that achieved by the lustre technique in which reduction is also often carried out during cooling.

It is unavoidable that ash from the burning material should leave marks in the soft glaze, and in the case of, say, wood-wool or straw, these marks look like greyish-black streaks in the cooled glaze. There will of course be times when this seems to spoil the total effect but in the vast majority of cases it will lend an extra quality to the robust form and the thick glaze.

One may argue about the value of these more or less incidental effects but even if control of glaze, firing etc. may be said to be essential in principle it is nevertheless true that in a number of areas many valuable details cannot be subject to control. We may mention as examples the results of traditional reducing firing, of salt glazing and many other processes the results of which cannot be foretold with 100 per cent certainty. But this does not prevent the articles produced being superior to other products, products that have been more carefully planned and controlled.

Under local reduction a change also takes place in the actual clay body, which assumes a darker, warmer colour. Clay with a content of iron oxides will often turn completely black and the body can form a pleasing contrast to the light glazes.

Bowl with thick lavender blue glaze, by Finn Lynggaard (1969). The marks left in the soft glaze by the iron tongs when the red-hot bowl is taken out of the kiln smooth themselves out in some cases, but in others, as here, help to give the bowl individuality.

Local reduction can be combined with cooling in water, and by using this method reduced glazes can sometimes be prevented from re-oxidizing on contact with the air.

The fired bowl is reduced first in the ordinary way in a metal container with a close-fitting lid.

When the reduction seems to be sufficient the bowl is taken out of the reduction bucket and dipped quickly into cold water.

Opposite
Under water cooling the clay becomes still more fragile and this violent process often results in the shapes cracking.

Local reduction causes violent smoking and should therefore be done in the open air.

Reduction by open firing

Another form of local reduction can be carried out after the articles have been removed from the kiln and cooled off in the normal way. A suitable number of articles are collected and stacked up, and a fire is lighted round them. The fuel may be paper, leaves, hay or branches and it has to be plentiful, so as to produce a great deal of smoke. With this method the temperature will be relatively low and the reduction not nearly so pronounced as with the preceding method in which the glaze was still red hot and fluid. Nevertheless, a slight change in the glaze will be noticeable, and the colour of the clay will be darkened as mentioned before. Unglazed articles decorated with a strip of various colours can be reduced in this way with advantage and a rich variety of tones will be achieved in the colour of the clay; the effect can be compared with early earthenware which was fired in an open fire.

Cooling in water

Finally I must mention a very radical method of cooling which consists of immersing the fired, red-hot article in a bucket of cold water as soon as it comes out of the kiln. The clay is made even more fragile by the violent shock and a crackling of the glaze is inevitable. For objects to bear cooling in this way it is essential for the clay to be specially fireproof and to have a grog content of about 50 per cent.

Water bowl for the tea ceremony, Japan (eighteenth century). During firing or cooling the bowl has cracked and the cracks have been filled with gold lacquer. (*Property of the Museum of Industrial Art, Copenhagen.*)

Firing

Open fire reduction is done *after* the articles are fired and cooled in the normal way. A suitable number of jars and bowls are stacked together and covered over with the fuel, which is generally hay, straw, dried leaves or any other material that will burn quickly and produce a lot of smoke.

Since the fuel-fired kiln is the most demanding purely from the point of view of time, the actual firing deserves a little more discussion. The fuel must be dry, well-seasoned wood cut into lengths that fit the firing tunnel which is 1–1½ in (3–4 cm) thick. In stoking it is not worth filling the tunnel full of fuel, but the pieces should be added slowly and steadily three or four at a time to get the best possible combustion and a constant rise in temperature. After a while as the glowing ashes pile up they are scraped away to the sides and the stoking continues in the centre of the tunnel. The ashes play their part in keeping the temperature at the same level and only ashes and material that has been completely consumed are scraped out to make way for fresh fuel.

When the kiln has reached maximum temperature and is heated well all through, the draught may be blocked a little by placing a couple of firebricks in front of the firing tunnel. From this moment onwards it will not be necessary to stoke as much as before in order to preserve the accumulated heat. As it will have taken from two to three hours to reach the desired temperature one should make the most of the heat while it lasts and have a good supply of glazed articles ready, so that the firing can continue for a long time. And 'a long time' can, as I know from experience, mean far into the light summer nights when one never grows weary of taking more and more things one by one out of the kiln.

We cannot know exactly what raku production meant in the Japan of long ago at social gatherings, when the guests shaped and fired their own tea-bowls and then drank tea out of them. But I know what it can mean in terms of inspiration and refreshment to a hardened potter to try out this simple medium which, with all its limitations, brings one right down to the basics. Its simple beauty can fill the craftsman with the same childish happiness that he felt the first time he held in his hands'a piece of pottery he had made himself.

Bowl with crater glaze, by
Finn Lynggaard (1968).

Glossary

Alkali glazes
Term for a group of glazes which contain substances such as calium, natrium and litium (possibly also calcium and magnesium). Turquoise glazes are generally of this type.

Ball clay
A fine grained, very plastic clay which with the addition of grog gives a fine, greyish white body.

Biscuit-fire
The first firing which serves to give the clay article a reasonable strength and porosity so that the body will be in a condition to absorb glaze.

Blue clay
A very plastic type of clay, common in Devon and Dorset and sold as Devonshire Ball Clay. After firing the clay takes on a light yellow colour.

Body
Term for the biscuit-fired or glost-fired clay mass.

Brushes
For decoration one should use long-haired, soft brushes such as the Japanese Sakura brushes which are both good and cheap.

Coloured slip
Slip coloured with oxide or pigment. Used for decoration on the raw, unfired body or for total colouring of this. Coloured slip can be applied by syringe, brush or by dipping.

Cones
Heat gauges in the form of small cones made out of the constituents of glazes. The cone is set in a small lump of clay and placed in the kiln in front of a peep-hole so that one can observe the cone and establish that the desired temperature has been

reached when the cone melts. Cones can be bought in 20° intervals from 60°C. upwards. There are three main brands of cone available in the U.K.; the Staffordshire Cone (made in England), the Seger Cone (made in West Germany) and the Orton Cone (made in America).

Contraction
The reduction in volume which the clay undergoes when changing from plastic to dry and later from dry to biscuit-fired clay. Contraction is given in per cent, calculated from the plastic to the biscuit-fired volume.

Drying
Evaporation of the mixing water of the plastic clay. Things which have not dried out before firing or glost-firing will be in danger of bursting during firing. One can guard against this by placing the piece to dry or warm up in the sun, close to a radiator or on top of the hot kiln.

Firebricks
Various qualities of high fired, fire resistant bricks which can stand temperatures of up to 1400–1600°C. are obtainable in the shops. They are quite expensive and are used for kilns of a more permanent nature.

Flux
The term covers materials which by virtue of their high fusibility are used to melt glazes together with other, less fusible substances or to reduce the melting point for a glaze of low fusibility. As far as raku is concerned, flux means substances such as red lead, borax, soda, calcium borate and many others.

Frit
Generic term for ready made products which are very useful for raku glazes. Frits are melted, ground products which include substances soluble in water, as for example soda and borax or other substances such as lead which in the form of a frit is almost free of poison. Lead frit is permitted in schools provided the soluble lead is below a definitely specified percentage.

Glost-firing
The second and last firing in which the clay particle after preliminary fire and glazing is fired to a melting temperature of the glaze.

Gold lacquer
A mixture of sealing wax and gold dust which the Japanese used to repair cracked tea bowls. The repair is visible and does not apparently affect the value the potter places on an otherwise successful bowl. In many cases it looks almost like a deliberate effect.

Ground glass
Commercial ground glass is obtainable in shops in various grades of fineness. The composition varies and test firings must be carried out in each individual case.

Iron tongs
A pair of tongs for raku use is not obtainable in the shops but can be made by a blacksmith to order. It is possible to make a pair oneself out of two pieces of round iron (about $\frac{1}{2}$ in or 1·3 cm); the tongs must be at least 2 ft (60 cm) long. Another possibility is simply to use a pair of grill tongs or old-fashioned tongs.

Lead carbonate
Also known as white lead and like red lead it is *poisonous*.

Lead glaze
Collective term for glazes in which the flux consists mainly of lead in the form of red lead which is *very poisonous*.

Lead poisoning
Red lead or lead carbonate can be absorbed through the skin or breathing system into the organism while one is working on them and so give rise to serious poisoning, possibly even permanent injury. As certain foodstuffs and drinks (for example tea) can dissolve parts of the glaze, glazes containing lead must *never* be used on articles that have a household function. Use instead a non-poisonous lead frit (*see frit*).

Leather-hard clay
When the clay at a certain point of time during drying has reached a stage at which it is still sufficiently moist to be able to be worked with a knife or scraper, one says that the clay is leather-hard.

Metallic salt
The result of metallic oxide plus acid. Salts are bought ready prepared, e.g. cobalt nitrate, copper sulphate, iron chloride, and these are used for the decoration of glazed objects. Metallic salts will give a softer and more fluid contour than oxides.

Moler bricks
Light insulating bricks of a certain fireproof character which makes them suitable for raku kilns for temperatures of up to 800–900°C.

Muffle
A container made of fireclay in which particles are placed during firing and which protects them from the direct effect of the flames.

Ochres, siennas and umbers
Natural earths containing greater or lesser quantities of iron oxide and manganese.

Open firing

The greenware articles are stacked on the ground and a bonfire built round them to which more and more fuel is added until the pieces are surrounded by flames and after 1–2 hours are red hot.

Oxides

Metallic oxides, for example iron, copper, manganese, cobalt, chromium can be used for the colouring of glaze or slip, or for under- or overglaze decoration.

Oxidization

A form of firing in which a balance is attempted between the combustion material and the supply of oxygen, which ensures a neutral atmosphere, i.e. an oxidising kiln atmosphere. In the case of firing in an electric kiln there is no question of combustion and the atmosphere will always be oxidizing unless combustion material is placed in the kiln chamber.

Porosity

The capacity of the clay to absorb glaze after preliminary firing.

Pyrometer

A measuring instrument consisting of a gauge and a case in which an indicator shows on a small scale the temperature inside the kiln.

Red clay

The commonest type of clay which is used for such articles as bricks, tiles, and flower pots. The clay is suitable for raku and takes on a particularly attractive colour under local reduction.

Red lead

Red lead, Pb_3O_4, is an excellent melting substance (flux) for low-firing kilns but its usefulness is limited owing to its being *highly poisonous*. Red lead must *never* be used in institutes or schools.

Reduction

A form of firing in which by cutting down the supply of oxygen for combustion a shortage of oxygen is created i.e. reducing kiln atmosphere.

Seger cones

(See cones.)

Sieves

Metal mesh mounted in a round wooden frame. Sieves are used for sieving the dissolved glaze and the holes should be quite fine; numbers 40–60 are suitable.

Size made up from Carragheen Moss
The recipe is as follows: boil two quarts of rainwater in a saucepan and when ready add 1 oz. of the moss. Boil for 5 minutes stirring all the time. After this take the saucepan from the fire and add any extra water required to bring to desired consistency.

Slip
Dried, pulverized clay which when stirred up with water forms a viscous liquid which is used to join leather-hard clay pieces.

Stoneware clay
Common term for many widely different types of clay. Common to almost all of them is the large content of kaolin and aluminium which means that stoneware clay can be fired at a very high temperature. The plasticity is generally less than with earthenware clay.

Talcum
Can be used in raku clay when great strength is desired; 5–15 per cent will have a useful effect but in general it is better to use talcum in conjunction with the usual addition of grog.

Tin glaze
Common term for ground glazes which with an addition of 5–10 per cent tin oxide have a white covering effect. Tin glazed articles are suitable for overglaze decoration.

Under- and overglaze colours
As the name indicates, there are colouring products, generally bought ready-made, which can be used for decoration under or over the glaze respectively.

Water cooling
Method of cooling by which the fired article is dipped in water immediately after firing. The violent shock crackles (cracks) the glaze and at the same time the clay becomes more fragile than usual.

Wax-resist
Method of decoration in which the clay article, after biscuit-firing, is decorated with hot, liquid wax applied by brush. In the subsequent glazing the wax will prevent the body absorbing the glaze, and after firing the areas covered remain plain.

Wood-firing
In general any dry wood may be said to be suitable for heating up a kiln. The fuel value varies greatly, however, with different kinds of wood, and the most economical results are obtained with dry beech, oak, thorn or juniper. The fuel is cut and then stored, often for up to two years, before being used.

Bibliography

Healey, Jean, 'Building a Raku Kiln'. *Ceramics Monthly* (October 1967)

Kakuzo, Okakuro, *The Book of Tea*. Vermont 1956

Leach, Bernard, *A Potter's Book*. London 1953

Leach, Bernard, *Kenzan and His Tradition*. London 1966

Miller, Roy Andrew, *Japanese Ceramics*. Tokyo 1961

Mitsouka, Tadanari, *Ceramic Art of Japan, vol 8*. Tokyo 1949

Nagumo, Ruy, *Japanese Pottery as a Hobby*. Tokyo 1963

Pageant of Japanese Art. Tokyo 1952

Rhodes, Daniel, *Kilns*. Philadelphia 1968

Riegger, Hal, 'Raku'. *Ceramics Monthly* (September, October, November 1965)

Riegger, Hal, *Raku*. New York 1970 (a VNR publication)

Sanders, Herbert H. *The World of Japanese Ceramics*. Tokyo 1967

Soldner, Paul, 'Firing with Oil'. *Craft Horizons*. (January, February 1968)

Yanagi, Soetsu, *Folk-Crafts in Japan*. Tokyo 1958

Index